S0-BZI-558

PALOS HEIGHTS PUBLIC LIBRARY

3 1965 00167 0642

Published by Creative Education
P.O. Box 227, Mankato, Minnesota 56002

Creative Education is an imprint of The Creative Company.
Design by Stephanie Blumenthal
Production design by Heidi Thompson
Art direction by Rita Marshall
Printed in the United States of America

Photographs by Ernest Hemingway Photograph Collection, John F. Kennedy
Presidential Library and Museum, Boston (Arnold Studios, Mary Hemingway);
Corbis (Archivo Iconografico, S.A.; Bettmann; John Bryson/Sygma; John
Springer Collection); Getty Images (Altrendo Travel; Lloyd Arnold/Hulton
Archive; Mary Kate Denny; Alfred Eisenstaidt/Life Magazine, Copyright Time
Inc./Time Life Pictures; Nat Farbman/Time & Life Pictures; Hulton Archive; Tore
Johnson/Pix Inc./Time Life Pictures; Keystone; Francis Miller//Time Life Pictures;
Francoise de Mulder/Roger Viollet; Herbert Orth//Time Life Pictures; Time &
Life Pictures; Time Life Pictures/Time Magazine,Copyright Time Inc./Time Life
Pictures); Jim Kerr Walloon Realty, LLC; The Granger Collection, New York
Text on page 42 from "The Nobel Prize in Literature 1954, Banquet Speech"
by Ernest Hemingway. © The Nobel Foundation 1954. Used by permission.

ERNEST

Interview excerpt on pages 42–45 from "The Art of Fiction: Ernest Hemingway,"
Ernest Hemingway interviewed by George Plimpton for *The Paris Review*
Writers at Work Series (Spring 1958) © Hemingway Foreign Rights Trust.
Abridged by permission of Scribner, an imprint of Simon & Schuster Adult
Publishing Group, on behalf of the Hemingway Foreign Rights Trust.

Copyright © 2009 Creative Education
International copyright reserved in all countries. No part of this book may be
reproduced in any form without written permission from the publisher.

Library of Congress Cataloging-in-Publication Data

Riggs, Kate.
Ernest Hemingway / by Kate Riggs.
p. cm. — (Xtraordinary artists)
Includes index.
ISBN 978-1-58341-661-7
1. Hemingway, Ernest, 1899–1961—Juvenile literature. 2. Authors. American—
20th century—Biography—Juvenile literature. I. Title. II. Series.

PS3515.E37Z758 2007
813'.52—dc22   2007004199

First edition

2 4 6 8 9 7 5 3 1

Palos Heights Public Library
12501 S. 71st Avenue
Palos Heights, IL 60463

J
BIO
HEMINGWAY

XTRAORDINARY ARTISTS

HEMINGWAY

KATE RIGGS

CREATIVE EDUCATION

he old man stood at his writing platform, relentlessly pounding the worn typewriter that was chest-high opposite him. His hair was grayer, and his eyes were less piercing than they had been. But he could still write. That much he could do. "I cannot write beautifully, but I can write with great accuracy (sometimes; I hope), and the accuracy makes a sort of beauty," he confided to a friend in 1953. Perhaps more than any other American writer of the early 20th century, Ernest Hemingway defined the modern era's notion of what it meant to be an author. And in doing so, the strapping, adventurous man who insisted upon being called "Papa" became a literary father to generations of American writers.

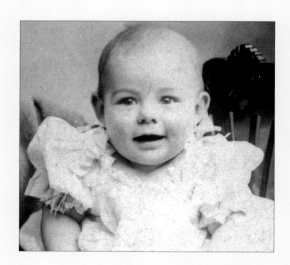

Ernest Miller Hemingway was born on July 21, 1899, the second child and oldest son in a family that would include four girls and two boys. In a sheltered suburb of Chicago, Illinois, called Oak Park, where Ernest was born, almost everyone came from a good family, and all were expected to live an honorable life—especially people named Hemingway. Ernest's father and mother, Dr. Clarence and Grace Hall Hemingway, came from highly respected families and never allowed their children to forget that. Although Ernest would eventually become best known for writing about his life experiences, he curiously never wrote about his youth in Oak Park: there is nothing in his later writing that speaks of growing up in a house with five siblings, of his mother singing in her studio, or of his father treating patients in his home office.

Hemingway had a great love of working on a typewriter; his first wife Hadley bought him his first machine when they moved to Paris in 1921

Playing the cello throughout his childhood was a way for Hemingway to keep his mother happy and daydream about story ideas at the same time

The Hemingway household, though, was full of music and creativity. Much of that atmosphere was due to his mother's love of the arts. Trained as an opera singer in New York before she married the doctor, Grace continued to use her musical skills when she returned to Oak Park by maintaining a studio of voice and piano students and instilling an appreciation of the arts in her children. She frequently took them to the opera, museums, and theater productions in the cultured city of Chicago. Although Ernest played the cello and sang in the church choir to appease his mother, his heart was not in the music itself; he used his cello practice time to think of stories that he would write down later.

"No sensible writer sets out deliberately to develop a style, but all writers do have distinguishing qualities, and they become very evident when you read the words. Take Hemingway, . . . [who] is extremely self-conscious and puts himself into every sentence and situation. . . . "

— *Essayist and critic E. B. White, on Hemingway's style*

Because of his mother, Ernest carried a love for fine art with him for the rest of his life. But he did not always appreciate his mother's influence. As he grew older and began to see what life was like for other Oak Park families, he began to resent the way her strong opinions on important subjects such as finances and religion dominated the household; Grace was the boss, but Ernest did not see such assertiveness in other Oak Park mothers. Other mothers were simply mothers. He wanted his mother to be like them.

Although as strong-willed as his mother, Ernest never recognized their striking similarities. They were both ambitious, artistic, stubborn, and intent upon getting their own

way. They both believed that they should be allowed to live their lives on their own terms. In the tender years of his youth, when Ernest most craved his father's guidance, it was his mother who served as the backbone of the family. He wanted to learn how to be a man, but his mother always seemed to get in the way. His father's personality was less assertive than his mother's, and he did not want to see his father that way.

During his early years, young "Ernie" trailed his father like a shadow, especially when they were involved in outdoor activities such as fishing, hunting, or hiking. Ernest intuited that honing his skills in these areas was part of becoming a man. Everything became a test

of manhood, and he would always feel that if an activity was not strenuous enough, it was not worth doing. But before Ernest reached his teen years, his father suddenly became disinterested in the pursuits they had once enjoyed. No one knew why. Looking back, Ernest may have realized it was a symptom of his father's losing battle against depression and anxiety, but at the time, the boy felt abandoned.

Ernest did what every other good Oak Park boy did: he obeyed his parents, participated in athletic events such as football, and did well enough in school to get by. He was not

Hemingway and his five siblings enjoyed their time on Lake Walloon, near Horton Bay, Michigan, spending their summer days swimming and playing

an exceptional child; even his boyish charm and dark, dancing eyes did not gain him many admirers outside his family at first. Among the close Hemingway clan, Ernie was the apple of his mother's eye and adored by his three younger sisters. But Ernest never put much stock in the biased affirmations of his family; he wanted to be noticed by girls who were not related to him. He also wanted to be taken seriously for his writing skill. By the time he reached high school, the seeds of his future career had been sown.

Around the time World War I began in 1914, when Ernest was only 15 years old, he began writing for his high school paper and discovered a love for journalism. But by the time the United States became involved in the global conflict in 1917, he was approaching 18 and was eager to enter the service. However, his parents were less enthusiastic and persuaded an uncle in Kansas to find Ernest a job as a reporter for the *Kansas City Star* instead.

Ernest remained at the *Star* for only a few months before he enlisted in the Red Cross's ambulance corps in 1918. (His poor eyesight prevented him from being able to serve

as a soldier.) Yet his time at the paper was not wasted; he learned quickly to test every experience to ensure its authenticity and developed a fine eye for observation. He listened intently to every conversation, lavishing his full attention on the speaker. Everyone who met Ernest was entranced by his ability to make them feel as if they were the most important person in the world—a technique that would serve him well in journalism and in love.

While in Italy driving ambulances and distributing rations to soldiers, Ernest also learned to entertain others with his stories and to hide his fears about the war. Both tricks proved useful after he was wounded by a trench mortar shell in July 1918 and sent to a hospital in Milan to heal. Restricted to bed rest and undergoing numerous surgeries to remove shrapnel from his legs, Ernest bided his time by entertaining the nurses and patients with

Hemingway drew from his experience of recovering in the Red Cross hospital in Milan when he wrote his 1929 novel A Farewell to Arms

13

When Hemingway was in his charm, but his cool façade could melt in a second, giving way to irrational bursts of anger

14

dramatic tales: Sometimes he had been hit by the shell and still managed to carry other soldiers to safety; other times he had simply blacked out from the pain. He was beginning to discover that he had a knack for fiction as well as reporting.

During this time, Ernest fell in love with his attractive American nurse, Agnes von Kurowsky. Agnes was eight years older, but she was flirtatious and talkative, and the two quickly formed an attachment. A year later, after Ernest had returned to America, he was heartbroken when he discovered that he had mistaken Agnes's ardent feelings for true love.

Back in Oak Park after the war, Ernest wished he could escape from the watchful eyes of his parents and neighbors. Having witnessed the brutality of war and fallen in love, he did not feel as though he belonged in the old-fashioned society of Oak Park. He was no longer a child, and the innocent, carefree days of his childhood were lost to him. He knew he could never go home, to the way things used to be.

"He is candid; he is highly skilled; he plants words precisely where he wishes; he has moments of bare and nervous beauty; he is modern in manner but not in vision; he is self-consciously virile; his talent has contracted rather than expanded."

— *British author Virginia Woolf*

So Ernest escaped into the world of fiction, trying to write serious stories that reflected the world as he now saw it. Since the right words did not come easily at first, he began imitating writers he admired, such as Ring Lardner, and styles that were popularly published. He was not yet ready to draw from his own life experience for fictional subject matter, so he sometimes turned to outdoor pastimes such as fishing and hunting and to sporting events such as boxing for ideas. Other times, Ernest would spend entire days at the Oak Park Public Library, devouring newspapers and popular magazines, hungry for tales of scandal and crime that he could rework into his own stories.

Yet Ernest's greatest source of inspiration was the forested land around Lake

Walloon, near Horton Bay, Michigan, where the Hemingways spent their summers through-

out Ernest's youth. This backwoods area would be the setting for some of his earliest pub-

lished short stories. But it would take Ernest more than 15 years to have such stories as

"Indian Camp" and "Big Two-Hearted River" published; it would take those years for him

to develop the elements that would become the definitive hallmarks of the Hemingway

style: the detached voice, the sense of ironic understatement, and the succinct encapsula-

tion of a truth. It would take his life experiences during the next decade to turn him into

the author who would become Ernest Hemingway.

The summer he turned 21, Ernest left Oak Park for good. He moved to Chicago, where he met two people who would prove instrumental in guiding his new, independent life: his first wife, Hadley Richardson, and author Sherwood Anderson.

Hadley, an educated, older woman of no profession, immediately fell under Ernest's riveting spell. Anderson, too, saw something in Ernest that intrigued him. As one of the great American short-story talents of the day, Anderson was the ideal person to introduce Ernest to Modernism and the literary landscape of the 20th century. It was a time of experimentation, and new trends were being set in language and literature.

Shortly after Ernest and Hadley were married in September 1921, they sailed to

France on Anderson's recommendation that Paris was the best place for modern artists to bloom. Ernest gained entrance into an elite circle of American expatriate poets and authors there, forming useful friendships with authors such as Ezra Pound, Gertrude Stein, and F. Scott Fitzgerald. Influenced by the expatriates, his training as a reporter, and the artistic atmosphere of 1920s Paris, Ernest finally found his voice.

In 1925, the 26-year-old made himself known to the world with the collection of short stories *In Our Time*. He was becoming an artist—and a tortured one at that. He had begun drinking heavily, which only made his erratic shifts in mood and angry outbursts more volatile. Such behavior was indicative of what would become a lifelong battle with depression,

Like many Parisians, Hemingway spent a great deal of time sitting at cafés, preferring to write there rather than in his and Hadley's cramped apartment

19

but at the time, Ernest's ready charm won him many more friends than he lost.

With his new friends, Ernest traveled throughout Europe, amassing experiences upon which he could base believable fiction. Whether he was tracking the bullfighting circuit in Spain, skiing in the Alps, or betting on horses and boxing matches in France, Ernest made every experience valid by writing about it. He wasn't ever merely having fun; he was always working, too. Ernest's first novel, *The Sun Also Rises* (1926), which chronicled a group of friends' exposure to Spanish bullfighting, showcased this philosophy so vividly that it put a strain on several relationships he had with the people who supplied the book's characters—his wife and their close friends.

"He was a complex, very difficult man with a tremendous zest for life, and when he did anything, he did it absolutely up to the hilt, no half measures.... Although I greatly admired him, I was always on guard because of his hair-trigger temper...."

—— *Tommy Shevlin, millionaire sportsman and fishing buddy of Hemingway*

Hemingway, pictured in 1934 with second wife Pauline Pfeiffer (top) and in 1941 with third wife Martha Gellhorn (bottom)

While working on the novel in 1925, Ernest had fallen in love with sophisticated *Vogue* editor and friend Pauline Pfeiffer. Although he had previously been devoted to Hadley, Ernest could not control his emotions where Pauline was concerned. A resigned Hadley granted him a divorce, and Ernest and Pauline were married in 1927. They moved to Key West, Florida, in 1928, the same year his father committed suicide—a sad end to the mental anguish that had long afflicted him.

Ernest then began working on a new novel, a book that would tell the story of his war and love experiences in Italy much more artfully than he could have done 10 years earlier. The critically and popularly acclaimed *A Farewell to Arms* was published in 1929 and catapulted Ernest into the league of America's best-selling authors.

Ernest used the 1930s to experiment with the form, subject matter, and style of his writing. With his terse dialogue and imagistic prose, he challenged the traditions of American literature and allowed others to do the same. During that transitional decade, he added marlin fishing and African safaris to his list of interests and acted as a correspondent during the Spanish Civil War. It was there that he met journalist Martha Gellhorn in 1937. For the second time, Ernest fell in love with another woman while married. By 1940, he had divorced and remarried once again.

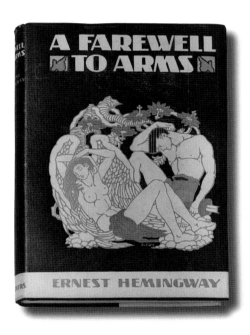

That year, Ernest's novel about the Spanish Civil War, *For Whom the Bell Tolls*, was hailed by *The New York Times* as "the best book Ernest Hemingway has written, the fullest, the deepest, the truest." He would not publish another book for 10 years, choosing instead to become heavily involved in the events of World War II and working on other projects. However, his competitive spirit was aroused when American author and writing rival William Faulkner received the Nobel Prize in Literature for 1949. Ernest was determined to show the world that he, too, was worthy of such an honor. He dove into a massive project that he would never complete but out of which would come a short, immortal novel.

As the scant light of dawn begins to illuminate the harbor, an old Cuban fisherman prepares his boat. He has not caught a fish in 84 days. But he has not lost faith—not yet. He is setting out alone in his small, rickety boat to catch a fish, any fish. After three days of intense struggle, he lands the biggest, most magnificent fish he has ever seen. The trip and the physical agony have been worth it. But then the old man sees the sharks. He watches as they circle menacingly around the fragile boat, drawn by the smell of blood in the water. The old man realizes that his beautiful fish, which is tied to the outside of the boat, is not going to survive the long journey back to port. He begins to lament that he has gone too far out to sea. He chastises himself for his foolishness. Yet he does not give up. He does not give in. He may be destroyed, but he will not be defeated.

Since moving to Key West in 1928, Ernest had become an avid fisherman, and he took frequent breaks from writing by going out to sea on his boat, the *Pilar*. He would fish any day that there were fish to be had, but Ernest was always most interested in capturing the biggest prize, such as the 18-foot (5.5 m) marlin featured in *The Old Man and the Sea*. During World War II, though, Ernest concentrated on fishing for enemy submarines and outfitted the *Pilar* as a spy boat. After the war, Ernest became enamored of the idea of writing a trilogy of connected novels, one about the sea of the Gulf Stream, one about the air, and one about the land, partly as a response to his wartime experiences in Cuba. He would spend the better

Hemingway prided himself on his fishing skill and often was not satisfied unless he got the biggest catch of the day among his boatmates

Hemingway met his Cuban friend Gregorio Fuentes (second from right) in 1928 and hired Fuentes to captain his boat for almost 30 years

part of 10 years on the daunting project, from which nothing but *The Old Man and the Sea* would be published during his lifetime. The chapter-less novella came from "The Sea Book." Its title character, an old man named Santiago, was modeled after Ernest's friend and longtime fishing mate Gregorio Fuentes.

Upon completing *The Old Man and the Sea*, which he continued to think of merely

as part of another, more unified book, Ernest was satisfied that it reflected his best work. On October 5, 1951, he wrote to his publisher, Charles Scribner, "This is the prose that I have been working for all my life that should read easily and simply and seem short and yet have all the dimensions of the visible world and the world of a man's spirit. It is as good prose as I can write as of now." Despite his early confidence, as the book's publishing date of

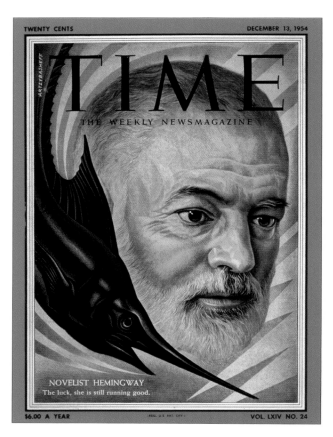

Labor Day, 1952, approached, Ernest grew more and more anxious about how other people would receive his little novel.

He need not have worried. The gray-haired Ernest may have looked like an old man by that time, but his prose in *The Old Man and the Sea* was anything but tired. It was vibrant and strong, and critics and general readers alike knew it. Six days after its initial publication in *Life* magazine, 50,000 copies of *The Old Man and the Sea* were published in book form and sold out within 10 days. By the end of the year, the little book had been translated into nine European languages and was igniting interest all over the world.

Ernest's poignant saga of the old fisherman Santiago's quest to capture a giant marlin earned him a Pulitzer Prize in 1953 and the Nobel Prize in Literature for 1954. Although some critics claimed that the awards came too late and for the wrong book, Ernest was

"[Hemingway] has no courage. He has never crawled out on a limb. He has never been known to use a word that might cause the reader to check with a dictionary to see if it is properly used."

— William Faulkner, one of Hemingway's biggest rivals

gratified and relieved. He was even uncharacteristically humble when first commenting on his reception of the Nobel Prize, saying that he would have been "happier...if the prize had been given to that beautiful writer Isak Dinesen," a Danish woman famous for her writings about Africa. He had finally achieved tangible recognition for his life's work, but he was not content to rest at the summit for long.

"Courage is Hemingway's central theme—the bearing of one who is put to the test and who steels himself to meet the cold cruelty of existence without, by so doing, repudiating the great and generous moments."

— *Anders Österling, Permanent Secretary of the Swedish Academy, the administrator of the Nobel Prizes, 1954*

The man who began calling himself "Papa" long before all three of his sons were born had, by 1940, become an authority figure in many arenas. And he knew it. Ernest had become his best publicist, making sure he was frequently interviewed or photographed. He reinvented the American public's perception of what it meant to be an author and cultivated a reputation of such magnitude that even he blurred the line between fiction and reality sometimes. Seldom did he give biographers the same answers to their questions about his life. His round, mustached face and burly physique, together with his daring exploits, made him one of the most recognizable and imitable figures of the era.

Living in their new home in Cuba called *Finca Vigía*, which is Spanish for "Lookout Farm," Ernest kept himself occupied while Martha was covering the events of World War II in Europe. He joined her in London in 1944. There he transferred his affections to another journalist, Mary Welsh, and divorced Martha.

After the success generated by *The Old Man and the Sea* in 1952, Ernest was inspired to write about another place he had loved since the 1930s: Africa. In August 1953, Ernest and Mary traveled there. The grueling, seven-month safari took a toll on Ernest's aging body, and he narrowly survived two airplane crashes near the safari's end.

As the 1950s progressed, so did Ernest's battle with depression. The political climate

Hemingway and his fourth wife, Mary Welsh, were together from 1946 until the end of his life, experiencing adventures such as a safari

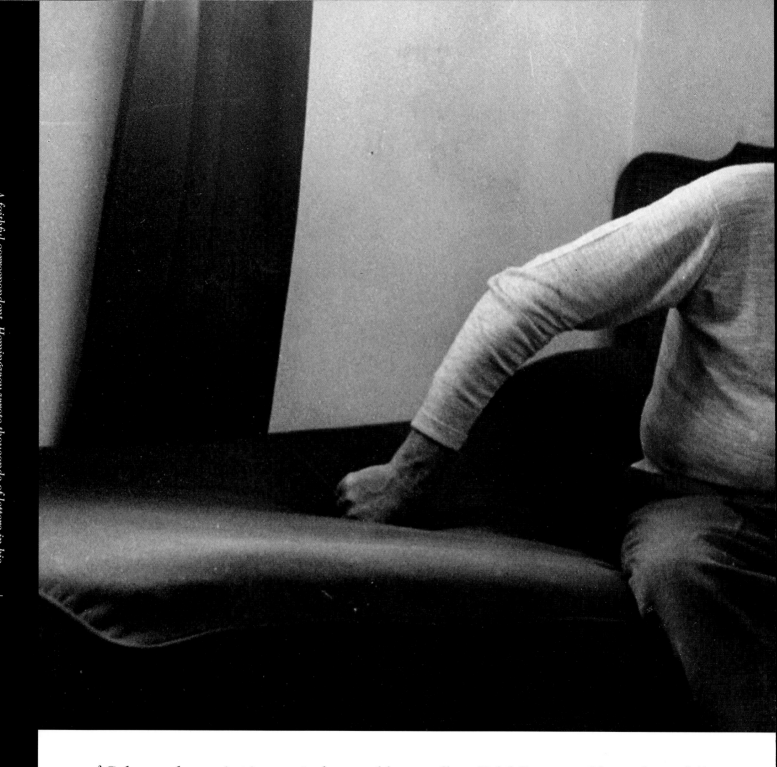

A faithful correspondent, Hemingway wrote thousands of letters in his lifetime, most of which are housed at Boston's John F. Kennedy Library

of Cuba was becoming increasingly unstable as well, as Fidel Castro and his militant followers continued to rage against the government. Just before Castro's communist forces took over in 1958, the Hemingways rented a house in Ketchum, Idaho, and prepared to start a new life there.

Soon after the escape to Ketchum, Ernest and Mary celebrated his 60th birthday. They did not know at the time that the last 30 months of Ernest's life would be his darkest.

Ernest became increasingly withdrawn, and the dark mood swings that had always been part of his temperament took over his personality completely. Yet for Ernest to admit that he was mentally ill would have meant that he had been defeated. To a man like Ernest, such a concession was unacceptable.

However, after seeing his haggard face on the cover of *Life* magazine in September 1960, Ernest realized that he did not look—or feel—like himself. At the end of November

1960, Ernest traveled to the Mayo Clinic in Rochester, Minnesota, to receive 10 sessions of electroconvulsive, or electroshock, therapy. The therapy involved stimulating the brain with electric currents, which had the effect of decreasing the symptoms of depression—at least in the short term.

The technique was not a guaranteed cure, but believing that he was better, doctors discharged Ernest on January 22, 1961, and the Hemingways returned to their house on the hill in Ketchum. There Ernest spent his time reading and taking long walks with Mary through the Idaho woods. Never a good sleeper, Ernest was waking early every day—and feeling desperate every day.

"I think you are more intelligent than this mss [manuscript]....
I want to say: me frien Hem, kin knock yew over the ropes;
and then I want to see the punch delivered. I dont want gentle
embraces in the middle of the ring."

— *Poet Ezra Pound, criticizing Hemingway's notebook writings*
in his unusual writing style

Ernest discovered that he was no longer able to write very much or very well. The man regarded as one of the greatest stylists of the English language could no longer put two coherent sentences together. He found it impossible to concentrate for any productive period of time, and his mind was a shroud of paranoia: he was consumed by money concerns and the idea that the Federal Bureau of Investigation (FBI) was pursuing him. Convinced he was no better, Mary pressed him to return to the Mayo Clinic in April 1961.

By the end of June, Hemingway persuaded the doctors—but not Mary—that he was fully recovered and ready to go home. Four days later, on June 30, they arrived back in

Ketchum, and Ernest appeared to be happier than he had been in a long time. But on the morning of Sunday, July 2, Ernest pulled on his slippers, retrieved his favorite double-barreled shotgun from the locked storeroom in the basement, walked back upstairs to the front foyer, and killed himself. At 7:30 A.M., the two shots awoke Mary from a sound sleep. Ernest Hemingway was dead, and the literary world had lost its father.

Hemingway loved cats and was especially fond of the unique polydactyl, or many-toed, variety; about 60 cats still live in his Key West home

41

"They don't realize that you can't win with Hemingway. He will give you an argument on anything, and he hates you just as much for arguing with him as he does for agreeing with him; and yet he can't reject the toadies."

— *American author and admirer John O'Hara*

Because of his injuries and continued illness following his 1953 African safari, Ernest Hemingway was unable to attend the Nobel Prize ceremonies in Stockholm, Sweden, on December 10, 1954. Instead, he submitted a written speech that was read by U.S. ambassador John C. Cabot. In the statement, Hemingway described the lonely life of an accomplished author, alluding to his own body of work as exceptional in form and style.

Having no facility for speech-making and no command of oratory nor any domination of rhetoric, I wish to thank the administrators of the generosity of Alfred Nobel for this Prize.

No writer who knows the great writers who did not receive the Prize can accept it other than with humility. There is no need to list these writers. Everyone here may make his own list according to his knowledge and his conscience.

It would be impossible for me to ask the Ambassador of my country to read a speech in which a writer said all of the things which are in his heart. Things may not be immediately discernible in what a man writes, and in this, sometimes, he is fortunate; but eventually they are quite clear and by these and a degree of alchemy that he possesses he will endure or be forgotten.

Writing, at its best, is a lonely life. Organizations for writers palliate the writer's loneliness but I doubt if they improve his writing. He grows in public stature as he sheds his loneliness and often his work deteriorates. For he does his work alone, and if he is a good enough writer he must face eternity, or the lack of it, each day.

For a true writer each book should be a new beginning where he tries again for something that is beyond attainment. He should always try for something that has never been done or that others have tried and failed. Then sometimes, with great luck, he will succeed.

How simple the writing of literature would be if it were only necessary to write in another way what has been well written. It is because we have had such great writers in the past that a writer is driven far out past where he can go, out to where no one can help him.

I have spoken too long for a writer. A writer should write what he has to say and not speak it. Again I thank you.

In the late 1950s, Hemingway was interviewed by numerous people, including George Plimpton, a representative of *The Paris Review*. Following are excerpts from a lengthy interview conducted by Plimpton at the author's home in Cuba. In it, Hemingway expounds on his writing habits and philosophies.

PLIMPTON (Q): *Are these hours during the actual process of writing pleasurable?*
HEMINGWAY (A): *Very.*

Q: *Could you say something of this process? When do you work? Do you keep to a strict schedule?*
A: *When I am working on a book or a story I write every morning as soon after first light as possible. There is no one to disturb you and it is cool or cold and you come to your work and warm as you write. You read what you have written and, as you always stop when you know what is going to happen next, you go on from there. You write until you come to a place where you still have your juice and know what will happen next and you stop and try to live through until the next day when you hit it again. You have started at six in the morning, say, and may go on until noon or be through before that.... Nothing can hurt you, nothing can happen, nothing means anything until the next day when you do it again. It is the wait until the next day that is hard to get through.*

Q: *Can you dismiss from your mind whatever project you're on when you're away from the typewriter?*
A: *Of course. But it takes discipline to do it and this discipline is acquired. It has to be.*

Q: *Do you do any rewriting as you read up to the place you left off the day before? Or does that come later, when the whole is finished?*
A: *I always rewrite each day up to the point where I stopped. When it is all finished, naturally you go over it. You get another chance to correct and rewrite when someone else types it, and you see it clean in type. The last chance is in the proofs. You're grateful for these different chances.*

Q: *How much rewriting do you do?*
A: *It depends. I rewrote the ending to* Farewell to Arms, *the last page of it, thirty-nine times before I was satisfied.*

Q: *Was there some technical problem there? What was it that had stumped you?*
A: *Getting the words right.*

Q: *Is it the rereading that gets the "juice" up?*

A: *Rereading places you at the point where it has to go on, knowing it is as good as you can get it up to there. There is always juice somewhere.*

Q: *But are there times when the inspiration isn't there at all?*

A: *Naturally. But if you stopped when you knew what would happen next, you can go on. As long as you can start, you are all right. The juice will come....*

Q: *Is emotional stability necessary to write well? You told me once that you could only write well when you were in love. Could you expound on that a bit more?*

A: *What a question. But full marks for trying. You can write any time people will leave you alone and not interrupt you. Or rather you can if you will be ruthless enough about it. But the best writing is certainly when you are in love. If it is all the same to you I would rather not expound on that.*

Q: *How about financial security? Can that be a detriment to good writing?*

A: *If it came early enough and you loved life as much as you loved your work it would take much character to resist the temptations. Once writing has become your major vice and greatest pleasure only death can stop it. Financial security then is a great help as it keeps you from worrying. Worry destroys the ability to write. Ill health is bad in the ratio that it produces worry which attacks your subconscious and destroys your reserves.*

Q: *Can you recall an exact moment when you decided to become a writer?*

A: *No, I always wanted to be a writer....*

Q: *How complete in your own mind is the conception of a short story? Does the theme, or the plot, or a character change as you go along?*

A: *Sometimes you know the story. Sometimes you make it up as you go along and have no idea how it will come out. Everything changes as it moves. That is what makes the movement which makes the story. Sometimes the movement is so slow it does not seem to be moving. But there is always change and always movement....*

Q: *So when you're not writing, you remain constantly the observer, looking for something which can be of use.*

A: *Surely. If a writer stops observing he is finished. But he does not have to observe consciously nor think how it will be useful. Perhaps that would be true at the beginning. But later everything he sees goes into the great reserve of things he knows or has seen. If it is any use to know it, I always try to write on the principle of the iceberg. There is seven-eighths of it underwater for every part that shows. Anything you know you can eliminate and it only strengthens your iceberg. It is the part that doesn't show. If a writer omits something because he does not know it then there is a hole in the story.*

The Old Man and the Sea could have been over a thousand pages long and had every character in the village in it and all the processes of how they made their living, were born, educated, bore children, etc. That is done excellently and well by other writers. In writing you are limited by what has already been done satisfactorily. So I have tried to learn to do something else. First I have tried to eliminate everything unnecessary to conveying experience to the reader so that after he or she has read something it will become a part of his or her experience and seem actually to have happened. This is very hard to do and I've worked at it very hard.

Anyway, to skip how it is done, I had unbelievable luck this time and could convey the experience completely and have it be one that no one had ever conveyed. The luck was that I had a good man and a good boy and lately writers have forgotten there still are such things. Then the ocean is worth writing about just as man is....

Q: Have you ever described any type of situation of which you had no personal knowledge?
A: That is a strange question. By personal knowledge do you mean carnal knowledge? In that case the answer is positive. A writer, if he is any good, does not describe. He invents or makes out of knowledge personal and impersonal and sometimes he seems to have unexplained knowledge which could come from forgotten racial or family experience. Who teaches the homing pigeon to fly as he does; where does a fighting bull get his bravery, or a hunting dog his nose?...

Q: Finally, a fundamental question: namely, as a creative writer, what do you think is the function of your art? Why a representation of fact, rather than the fact itself?
A: Why be puzzled by that? From things that have happened and from things as they exist and from all things that you know and all those you cannot know, you make something through your invention that is not a representation but a whole new thing truer than anything true and alive, and you make it alive, and if you make it well enough, you give it immortality. That is why you write and for no other reason that you know of. But what about all the reasons that no one knows?

1899

Ernest Miller Hemingway is born in Oak Park, Illinois, on July 21.

1917

Hemingway works for the Kansas City Star for seven months before enlisting as a World War I ambulance driver.

1918

Hemingway is wounded by a trench mortar shell while passing out provisions to Italian soldiers.

1920

Hemingway works for a farming journal called Cooperative Commonwealth in Chicago.

1921

Hemingway marries wealthy St. Louis native Hadley Richardson. They sail for France in December.

1923

Hemingway's first son, John, is born; two more sons (Patrick and Gregory) will follow in 1928 and 1931.

1925

Hemingway travels to Spain for the second time to follow the summer bullfights.

1928

Hemingway moves to Key West, Florida, with his second wife, Pauline; his father commits suicide.

1931

A Farewell to Arms, Hemingway's novel about his experiences in World War I, is published.

1937

Hemingway supports the cause of those who opposed dictator Francisco Franco while witnessing the Spanish Civil War.

1940

Martha Gellhorn and Hemingway marry, and For Whom the Bell Tolls is published.

1944

Hemingway begins a relationship with journalist Mary Welsh, and they marry two years later.

1952

Hemingway's novella The Old Man and the Sea marks his triumphal return to the forefront of American literature.

1954

Several American newspapers mistakenly report Hemingway's death after he is involved in two plane crashes in Africa.

1957

Two trunks of Hemingway's 1920s writing are found; he begins writing his memoir, A Moveable Feast.

1959

The Hemingways purchase a home in Ketchum, Idaho, then travel to Spain to follow the summer bullfights.

1960

Hemingway continues to work but sinks into depression; he goes to the Mayo Clinic in November for treatment.

1961

Shortly before turning 62, Hemingway commits suicide at his home in Ketchum.

Communist — A person who believes in—or something relating to—communism, a social system that is characterized by the state's ownership of and control over all aspects of life

electroconvulsive therapy — An electricity-based treatment for the mentally ill that was commonplace among psychiatrists from the 1930s through the late 20th century but which became increasingly controversial over time

expatriate — A person who lives outside his or her native country, as many American artists and authors did during the first half of the 20th century

Ezra Pound — An influential American poet, critic, and editor of the early 20th century who championed the work of many aspiring authors of the day and belonged to Gertrude Stein's exclusive circle in Paris

F. Scott Fitzgerald — An American novelist and short-story writer best known for his works of the 1920s such as This Side of Paradise, Tales of the Jazz Age, and The Great Gatsby

Fidel Castro — A leader of the Cuban Revolution who became prime minister of the country after overthrowing Fulgencio Batista; he became Cuban president in 1976, when he made the Communist party the country's only legal party

Gertrude Stein — An American poet and novelist who was at the center of the Modernist movement in Paris during the early 20th century and influenced the careers of many young authors and artists

Modernism — An artistic movement in the early 1900s concerned with breaking from traditional forms in art and literature and finding new methods of expression for the future

Nobel Prize in Literature — An annual, international award established in 1901 by Swedish benefactor Alfred Nobel to honor an author's exceptional and influential work

Sherwood Anderson — An American novelist and short-story writer best known for his 1919 collection Winesburg, Ohio; he influenced the writing and careers of such authors as Hemingway, William Faulkner, and John Steinbeck

Spanish Civil War — The war, from 1936 to 1939, between fascist powers and the established Spanish republican government that ended with General Francisco Franco's dictatorial government winning control of the country

World War I — The war fought in Europe from 1914 to 1918 between the Allied Powers (France, Russia, Great Britain, Italy, and the U.S.) and the Central Powers (Austria-Hungary, Germany, Bulgaria, and the Ottoman Empire)

World War II — A worldwide conflict that involved more than 70 nations; the war was instigated by German dictator Adolf Hitler in 1939 and ended in 1945 with the defeat of Germany, Italy, and Japan

Africa 23, 32

Anderson, Sherwood 18

birth 4

bullfighting 20

Chicago, Illinois 4, 6, 18

childhood 4, 6, 8–10, 12, 17

   music 6

   outdoor pursuits 9–10

   writing 6, 11, 12

      journalism 12

Cuba 24, 32, 34

death 40

depression 20, 32, 35–36, 38, 40

drinking 18

family

   Hemingway, Clarence (father) 4, 6, 8, 9, 10, 22

      depression 10

   Hemingway, Grace Hall (mother) 4, 6, 8–9, 10

Faulkner, William 23, 29

fishing 9, 16, 23, 24

Fitzgerald, F. Scott 18

Fuentes, Gregorio 26

hunting 9, 16, 23

Italy 12, 22

Kansas City Star 12

Ketchum, Idaho 34, 36, 40

Key West, Florida 22, 24

Kurowsky, Agnes von 14

Lardner, Ring 16

Mayo Clinic 36, 38

Michigan 16–17

   Lake Walloon 16–17

Modernism 18

Nobel Prize in Literature 23, 28, 30, 42

Oak Park, Illinois 4, 8, 10, 14, 18

Paris, France 18

Pound, Ezra 18, 37

Pulitzer Prize 28

Spain 20, 23

sports 16, 20

Stein, Gertrude 18

wives

   Gellhorn, Martha (third) 23, 32

   Pfeiffer, Pauline (second) 22

   Richardson, Hadley (first) 18, 22

   Welsh, Mary (fourth) 32, 34, 36, 38, 40

works

   "Big Two-Hearted River" 17

   A Farewell to Arms 23

   For Whom the Bell Tolls 23

   In Our Time 18

   "Indian Camp" 17

   The Old Man and the Sea 24, 26–28, 30, 32

   The Sun Also Rises 20

World War I 12

World War II 23, 24, 32

writing style 7, 16, 17, 23

Baker, Carlos, ed. *Ernest Hemingway: Selected Letters, 1917–1961.* New York: Charles Scribner's Sons, 1981.

Bruccoli, Matthew J., with Judith S. Baughman. *Hemingway and the Mechanism of Fame.* Columbia, S.C.: University of South Carolina Press, 2006.

Plimpton, George, ed. "Ernest Hemingway: An Interview." *Writers at Work,* The Paris Review *Interviews,* Vol. 2. New York: Viking Press, 1963.

Reynolds, Michael. *The Young Hemingway.* Oxford: Basil Blackwell, 1986. Vol. 1

———. *Hemingway: The Paris Years.* Oxford: Basil Blackwell, 1989. Vol. 2

———. *Hemingway: The American Homecoming.* Oxford: Basil Blackwell, 1992. Vol. 3

———. *Hemingway: The 1930s.* New York: Norton, 1997. Vol. 4

———. *Hemingway: The Final Years.* New York: Norton, 1999. Vol. 5